Machines That Work

Big Bulldozers

Amy Hayes

Cavendish Square

New York

Published in 2016 by Cavendish Square Publishing, LLC
243 5th Avenue, Suite 136, New York, NY 10016

Copyright © 2016 by Cavendish Square Publishing, LLC

First Edition

Website: cavendishsq.com

This publication represents the opinions and views of the author based on his or her personal experience, knowledge, and research. The information in this book serves as a general guide only. The author and publisher have used their best efforts in preparing this book and disclaim liability rising directly or indirectly from the use and application of this book.

CPSIA Compliance Information: Batch #WS15CSQ

All websites were available and accurate when this book was sent to press.

Library of Congress Cataloging-in-Publication Data

Hayes, Amy, author.
Big bulldozers / Amy Hayes.
pages cm. — (Machines that work)
Includes index.
ISBN 978-1-50260-389-0 (hardcover)
ISBN 978-1-50260-388-3 (paperback)
ISBN 978-1-50260-390-6 (ebook)
1. Bulldozers—Juvenile literature. 2. Earthmoving machinery—Juvenile literature. I. Title.

TA735.H393 2016
629.225—dc23

2014049215

Editorial Director: David McNamara
Copy Editor: Cynthia Roby
Art Director: Jeffrey Talbot
Designer: Stephanie Flecha
Senior Production Manager: Jennifer Ryder-Talbot
Production Editor: Renni Johnson

Printed in the United States of America

Contents

Bulldozers are big machines.

4

5

Bulldozers have a big **blade** called a plate.

7

The plate pushes rocks
and dirt.

9

Bulldozers can push dirt
into big piles.

11

In the back of some bulldozers, there is a **ripper**.

A ripper can break apart hard surfaces.

13

The ripper has a **shank**.

The shank pushes into the ground to break it apart.

15

Some bulldozers have big chains that help them move.

These bulldozers are called **crawlers**.

17

Operating a bulldozer is hard work!

There are lots of controls to use.

18

Bulldozers are great!

They are always busy
working hard.

21

New Words

blade (BLAYD) The wide, curved part at the front of a bulldozer.

crawler (CRAW-lr) A bulldozer that has chains to help it move.

operating (OP-er-ayt-ing) Working in the proper way.

ripper (RIP-pur) A machine used to break up material.

shank (SHANK) The straight, narrow part of a ripper that goes into the ground.

Index

23

About the Author

Amy Hayes lives in the beautiful city of Buffalo, New York. She has written several books for children, including the Machines That Work and the Our Holidays series for Cavendish Square.

About BOOKWORMS

Bookworms help independent readers gain reading confidence through high-frequency words, simple sentences, and strong picture/text support. Each book explores a concept that helps children relate what they read to the world in which they live.